WOMEN WHO FINISH

MY WEEKLY & QUARTERLY PROJECT PLANNER

WomenWhoFinish.com

"But I do not account my life of any value nor as precious to myself, **if only I may finish my course** and the ministry that I received from the Lord Jesus, to testify to the gospel of the grace of God."

– Acts 20:24

DON'T JUST PLAN THE WORK, WORK THE PLAN.

WHERE DO I WANT TO BE IN ONE YEAR:

_____

_____

_____

_____

_____

_____

_____

_____

_____

_____

_____

_____

_____

_____

_____

_____

_____

SKETCH, DREAM, IMAGINE:

_____

_____

_____

_____

_____

_____

_____

_____

_____

_____

_____

_____

_____

_____

_____

_____

_____

BE MORE SPECIFIC, CHOOSE 3 PROJECTS TO MAKE NON-NEGOTIABLE* THIS YEAR:

*Need help deciding?
Visit **Robyn-Ann.com/decide** for the 3 essential questions to ask yourself first.

PRAY FOR HOW TO PRIORITIZE EACH PROJECT, THEN ASSIGN A FOCUS TO EACH QUARTER: [WATCH OUT FOR MONTHS OCT - DEC WHICH BRING LOTS OF HOLIDAYS, INTERRUPTIONS, AND FAMILY GATHERINGS]

QUARTER 1

QUARTER 2

QUARTER 3

QUARTER 4

LORD, WHAT DO I NEED TO REMEMBER WHEN THINGS GET TOUGH:

_____

_____

_____

_____

_____

_____

_____

_____

_____

_____

_____

_____

_____

_____

_____

_____

_____

_____

PRAYERS & PROMISES TO TRACK FOR THE YEAR AHEAD:

_____

_____

_____

_____

_____

_____

_____

_____

_____

_____

_____

_____

_____

_____

_____

_____

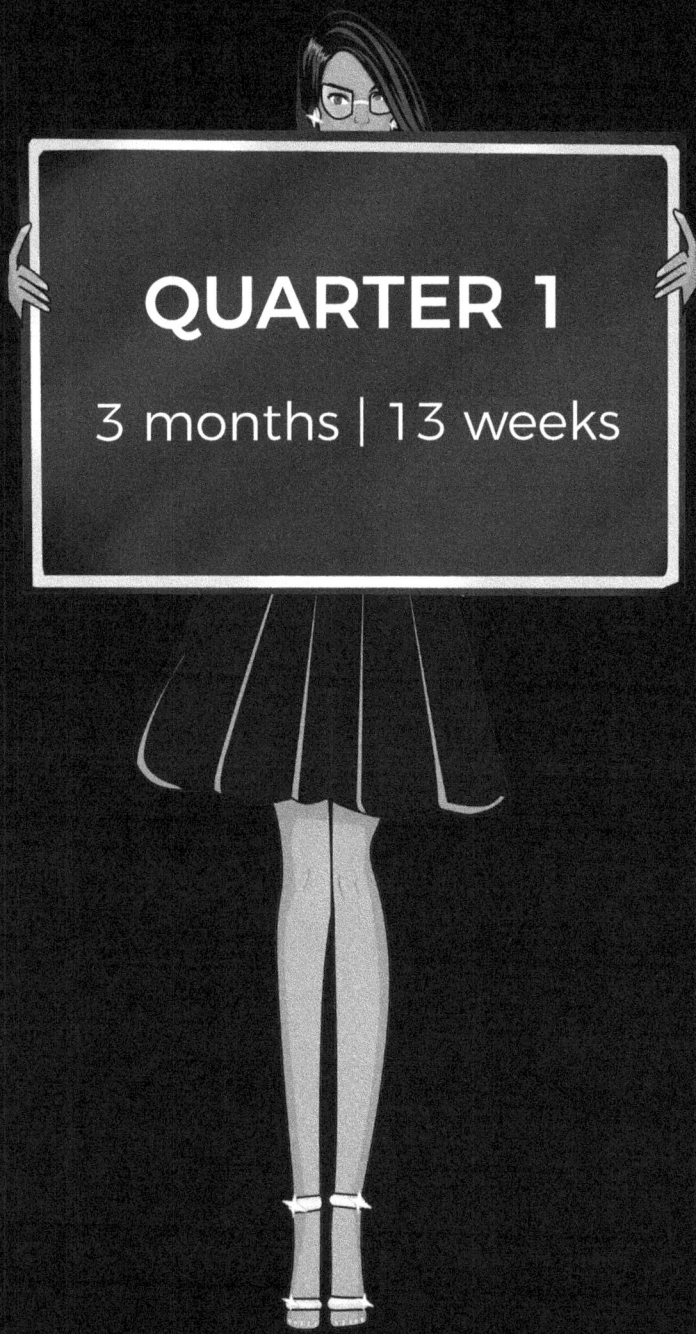

QUARTER 1

3 months | 13 weeks

QUARTER 1 - MY RESOLUTION TO FINISH

God has stirred my heart & asked me to create: (THE CALL)

So this quarter I will prioritize: (THE WHAT)

I need to finish this because: (THE WHY)

I cannot **make** time so I will **take** time from: (THE HOW)

I will set aside non-negotiable time to do this on: (THE WHEN)

To minimize distractions, I will go do this at: (THE WHERE)

To get accountability and snitch on my excuses, I will tell: (THE WHO)

Once this is done, I will finally feel: (THE WIN)

THIS QUARTER'S PROJECT:

I will complete _____

by _____

PROJECT DUMP: (LIST ALL POSSIBLE TASKS)

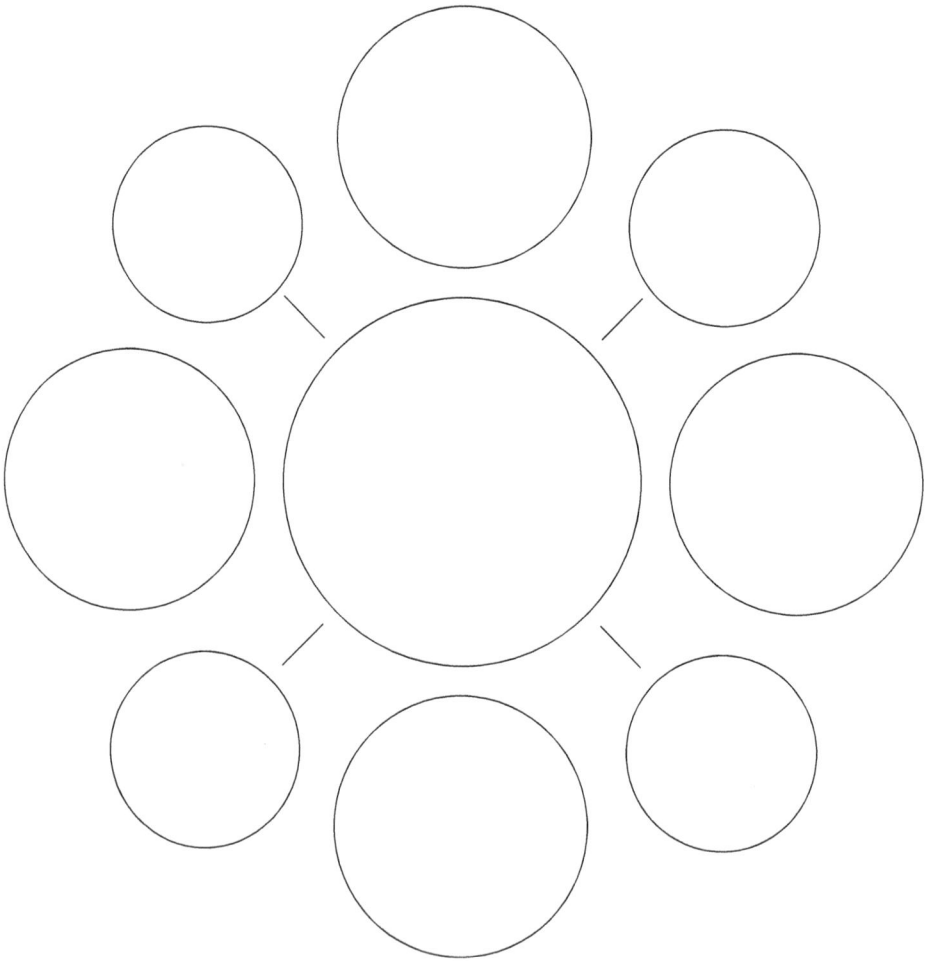

THIS QUARTER'S PRIORITIES

(ASSIGN ESSENTIAL TASKS TO A SPECIFIC MONTH)

MONTH 1:

MONTH 2:

MONTH 3:

ITEMS TO FINISH FIRST:

1. _____

2. _____

3. _____

4. _____

5. _____

NOTES

_____

_____

_____

_____

_____

_____

_____

Show me the way
I should go, for to
you I entrust my
life.

Psalm 143:8

Month 1

SUNDAY	MONDAY	TUESDAY

WEDNESDAY	THURSDAY	FRIDAY	SATURDAY

THIS WEEK, I'M THANKFUL THAT I GET TO:

3 THINGS TO FINISH THIS WEEK:

MONDAY

PRIORITIES

_____
_____
_____
_____

TUESDAY

PRIORITIES

_____
_____
_____
_____
_____

WEDNESDAY

PRIORITIES

_____
_____
_____
_____

FUEL TO FINISH: (PRAYERS, SCRIPTURE, MEMOS TO SELF...)

THURSDAY

PRIORITIES

_____
_____
_____
_____
_____

FRIDAY

PRIORITIES

_____
_____
_____
_____
_____

SATURDAY

SUNDAY

WEEKLY REFLECTION

HOW DID I FEEL ABOUT THIS WEEK?

ONE AMAZING THING THAT HAPPENED?

WHAT WILL I DO BETTER/DIFFERENTLY NEXT WEEK?

THINGS TO PRAY ABOUT (& NOT WORRY ABOUT)?

WHY DO I STILL NEED TO FINISH WHAT I STARTED?

NEW IDEAS, WISDOM, MINDSET SHIFTS:

_____

_____

_____

_____

_____

_____

_____

_____

_____

_____

_____

_____

_____

_____

_____

_____

_____

_____

_____

_____

THIS WEEK, I'M THANKFUL THAT I GET TO:

3 THINGS TO FINISH THIS WEEK:

MONDAY

	PRIORITIES
	_____
	_____
	_____
	_____

TUESDAY

	PRIORITIES
	_____
	_____
	_____
	_____

WEDNESDAY

	PRIORITIES
	_____
	_____
	_____
	_____

FUEL TO FINISH: (PRAYERS, SCRIPTURE, MEMOS TO SELF...)

THURSDAY

PRIORITIES

FRIDAY

PRIORITIES

SATURDAY

SUNDAY

WEEKLY REFLECTION

HOW DID I FEEL ABOUT THIS WEEK?

ONE AMAZING THING THAT HAPPENED?

WHAT WILL I DO BETTER/DIFFERENTLY NEXT WEEK?

THINGS TO PRAY ABOUT (& NOT WORRY ABOUT)?

WHY DO I STILL NEED TO FINISH WHAT I STARTED?

NEW IDEAS, WISDOM, MINDSET SHIFTS:

_____

_____

_____

_____

_____

_____

_____

_____

_____

_____

_____

_____

_____

_____

_____

_____

_____

_____

THIS WEEK, I'M THANKFUL THAT I GET TO:

3 THINGS TO FINISH THIS WEEK:

MONDAY

PRIORITIES

TUESDAY

PRIORITIES

WEDNESDAY

PRIORITIES

FUEL TO FINISH: (PRAYERS, SCRIPTURE, MEMOS TO SELF...)

THURSDAY

PRIORITIES

_____
_____
_____
_____

FRIDAY

PRIORITIES

_____
_____
_____
_____

SATURDAY

SUNDAY

WEEKLY REFLECTION

HOW DID I FEEL ABOUT THIS WEEK?

ONE AMAZING THING THAT HAPPENED?

WHAT WILL I DO BETTER/DIFFERENTLY NEXT WEEK?

THINGS TO PRAY ABOUT (& NOT WORRY ABOUT)?

WHY DO I STILL NEED TO FINISH WHAT I STARTED?

NEW IDEAS, WISDOM, MINDSET SHIFTS:

_____

_____

_____

_____

_____

_____

_____

_____

_____

_____

_____

_____

_____

_____

_____

_____

_____

_____

_____

_____

THIS WEEK, I'M THANKFUL THAT I GET TO:

3 THINGS TO FINISH THIS WEEK:

MONDAY

PRIORITIES

TUESDAY

PRIORITIES

WEDNESDAY

PRIORITIES

FUEL TO FINISH: (PRAYERS, SCRIPTURE, MEMOS TO SELF...)

THURSDAY

PRIORITIES

FRIDAY

PRIORITIES

SATURDAY

SUNDAY

WEEKLY REFLECTION

HOW DID I FEEL ABOUT THIS WEEK?

ONE AMAZING THING THAT HAPPENED?

WHAT WILL I DO BETTER/DIFFERENTLY NEXT WEEK?

THINGS TO PRAY ABOUT (& NOT WORRY ABOUT)?

WHY DO I STILL NEED TO FINISH WHAT I STARTED?

NEW IDEAS, WISDOM, MINDSET SHIFTS:

Month **2**

1. _____

2. _____

3. _____

4. _____

5. _____

NOTES

_____

_____

_____

_____

_____

_____

_____

_____

Finishing is better
than starting.
Patience is better
than pride.

Ecclesiastes 7:8

SUNDAY	MONDAY	TUESDAY

WEDNESDAY	THURSDAY	FRIDAY	SATURDAY

THIS WEEK, I'M THANKFUL THAT I GET TO:

3 THINGS TO FINISH THIS WEEK:

MONDAY

PRIORITIES

TUESDAY

PRIORITIES

WEDNESDAY

PRIORITIES

FUEL TO FINISH: (PRAYERS, SCRIPTURE, MEMOS TO SELF...)

THURSDAY

PRIORITIES

FRIDAY

PRIORITIES

SATURDAY

SUNDAY

WEEKLY REFLECTION

HOW DID I FEEL ABOUT THIS WEEK?

ONE AMAZING THING THAT HAPPENED?

WHAT WILL I DO BETTER/DIFFERENTLY NEXT WEEK?

THINGS TO PRAY ABOUT (& NOT WORRY ABOUT)?

WHY DO I STILL NEED TO FINISH WHAT I STARTED?

NEW IDEAS, WISDOM, MINDSET SHIFTS:

THIS WEEK, I'M THANKFUL THAT I GET TO:

3 THINGS TO FINISH THIS WEEK:

MONDAY

PRIORITIES

TUESDAY

PRIORITIES

WEDNESDAY

PRIORITIES

FUEL TO FINISH: (PRAYERS, SCRIPTURE, MEMOS TO SELF...)

THURSDAY

PRIORITIES

_____

_____

_____

_____

_____

FRIDAY

PRIORITIES

_____

_____

_____

_____

_____

SATURDAY

SUNDAY

WEEKLY REFLECTION

HOW DID I FEEL ABOUT THIS WEEK?

ONE AMAZING THING THAT HAPPENED?

WHAT WILL I DO BETTER/DIFFERENTLY NEXT WEEK?

THINGS TO PRAY ABOUT (& NOT WORRY ABOUT)?

WHY DO I STILL NEED TO FINISH WHAT I STARTED?

NEW IDEAS, WISDOM, MINDSET SHIFTS:

THIS WEEK, I'M THANKFUL THAT I GET TO:

3 THINGS TO FINISH THIS WEEK:

MONDAY

PRIORITIES

TUESDAY

PRIORITIES

WEDNESDAY

PRIORITIES

FUEL TO FINISH: (PRAYERS, SCRIPTURE, MEMOS TO SELF...)

THURSDAY

PRIORITIES

_____
_____
_____
_____

FRIDAY

PRIORITIES

_____
_____
_____
_____

SATURDAY

SUNDAY

WEEKLY REFLECTION

HOW DID I FEEL ABOUT THIS WEEK?

ONE AMAZING THING THAT HAPPENED?

WHAT WILL I DO BETTER/DIFFERENTLY NEXT WEEK?

THINGS TO PRAY ABOUT (& NOT WORRY ABOUT)?

WHY DO I STILL NEED TO FINISH WHAT I STARTED?

NEW IDEAS, WISDOM, MINDSET SHIFTS:

_____

_____

_____

_____

_____

_____

_____

_____

_____

_____

_____

_____

_____

_____

_____

_____

_____

_____

_____

_____

_____

THIS WEEK, I'M THANKFUL THAT I GET TO:

3 THINGS TO FINISH THIS WEEK:

MONDAY

PRIORITIES
_____
_____
_____
_____

TUESDAY

PRIORITIES
_____
_____
_____
_____

WEDNESDAY

PRIORITIES
_____
_____
_____
_____

FUEL TO FINISH: (PRAYERS, SCRIPTURE, MEMOS TO SELF...)

THURSDAY

PRIORITIES

_____
_____
_____
_____

FRIDAY

PRIORITIES

_____
_____
_____
_____

SATURDAY

SUNDAY

WEEKLY REFLECTION

HOW DID I FEEL ABOUT THIS WEEK?

ONE AMAZING THING THAT HAPPENED?

WHAT WILL I DO BETTER/DIFFERENTLY NEXT WEEK?

THINGS TO PRAY ABOUT (& NOT WORRY ABOUT)?

WHY DO I STILL NEED TO FINISH WHAT I STARTED?

NEW IDEAS, WISDOM, MINDSET SHIFTS:

_____

_____

_____

_____

_____

_____

_____

_____

_____

_____

_____

_____

_____

_____

_____

_____

_____

_____

_____

THIS WEEK, I'M THANKFUL THAT I GET TO:

3 THINGS TO FINISH THIS WEEK:

MONDAY

PRIORITIES

_____
_____
_____
_____

TUESDAY

PRIORITIES

_____
_____
_____
_____

WEDNESDAY

PRIORITIES

_____
_____
_____
_____

FUEL TO FINISH: (PRAYERS, SCRIPTURE, MEMOS TO SELF...)

THURSDAY

PRIORITIES

FRIDAY

PRIORITIES

SATURDAY

SUNDAY

WEEKLY REFLECTION

HOW DID I FEEL ABOUT THIS WEEK?

ONE AMAZING THING THAT HAPPENED?

WHAT WILL I DO BETTER/DIFFERENTLY NEXT WEEK?

THINGS TO PRAY ABOUT (& NOT WORRY ABOUT)?

WHY DO I STILL NEED TO FINISH WHAT I STARTED?

NEW IDEAS, WISDOM, MINDSET SHIFTS:

_____

_____

_____

_____

_____

_____

_____

_____

_____

_____

_____

_____

_____

_____

_____

_____

_____

_____

1. _____

2. _____

3. _____

4. _____

5. _____

Month **3**

SUNDAY	MONDAY	TUESDAY

NOTES

_____

_____

_____

_____

_____

_____

_____

The mind of man plans his way, but the Lord directs his steps.

Proverbs 16:9

WEDNESDAY	THURSDAY	FRIDAY	SATURDAY

THIS WEEK, I'M THANKFUL THAT I GET TO:

3 THINGS TO FINISH THIS WEEK:

MONDAY

PRIORITIES

_____
_____
_____
_____
_____

TUESDAY

PRIORITIES

_____
_____
_____
_____
_____

WEDNESDAY

PRIORITIES

_____
_____
_____
_____

FUEL TO FINISH: (PRAYERS, SCRIPTURE, MEMOS TO SELF...)

THURSDAY

PRIORITIES
_____
_____
_____
_____
_____

FRIDAY

PRIORITIES
_____
_____
_____
_____
_____

SATURDAY

SUNDAY

WEEKLY REFLECTION

HOW DID I FEEL ABOUT THIS WEEK?

ONE AMAZING THING THAT HAPPENED?

WHAT WILL I DO BETTER/DIFFERENTLY NEXT WEEK?

THINGS TO PRAY ABOUT (& NOT WORRY ABOUT)?

WHY DO I STILL NEED TO FINISH WHAT I STARTED?

NEW IDEAS, WISDOM, MINDSET SHIFTS:

_____

_____

_____

_____

_____

_____

_____

_____

_____

_____

_____

_____

_____

_____

_____

_____

_____

_____

_____

_____

THIS WEEK, I'M THANKFUL THAT I GET TO:

3 THINGS TO FINISH THIS WEEK:

MONDAY

PRIORITIES

TUESDAY

PRIORITIES

WEDNESDAY

PRIORITIES

FUEL TO FINISH: (PRAYERS, SCRIPTURE, MEMOS TO SELF...)

THURSDAY

PRIORITIES

FRIDAY

PRIORITIES

SATURDAY

SUNDAY

WEEKLY REFLECTION

HOW DID I FEEL ABOUT THIS WEEK?

ONE AMAZING THING THAT HAPPENED?

WHAT WILL I DO BETTER/DIFFERENTLY NEXT WEEK?

THINGS TO PRAY ABOUT (& NOT WORRY ABOUT)?

WHY DO I STILL NEED TO FINISH WHAT I STARTED?

NEW IDEAS, WISDOM, MINDSET SHIFTS:

_____

_____

_____

_____

_____

_____

_____

_____

_____

_____

_____

_____

_____

_____

_____

_____

_____

_____

_____

THIS WEEK, I'M THANKFUL THAT I GET TO:

3 THINGS TO FINISH THIS WEEK:

MONDAY

PRIORITIES

_____
_____
_____
_____

TUESDAY

PRIORITIES

_____
_____
_____
_____
_____

WEDNESDAY

PRIORITIES

_____
_____
_____
_____
_____

WomenWhoFinish.com

FUEL TO FINISH: (PRAYERS, SCRIPTURE, MEMOS TO SELF...)

THURSDAY

PRIORITIES

_____
_____
_____
_____
_____

FRIDAY

PRIORITIES

_____
_____
_____
_____
_____

SATURDAY

SUNDAY

WEEKLY REFLECTION

HOW DID I FEEL ABOUT THIS WEEK?

ONE AMAZING THING THAT HAPPENED?

WHAT WILL I DO BETTER/DIFFERENTLY NEXT WEEK?

THINGS TO PRAY ABOUT (& NOT WORRY ABOUT)?

WHY DO I STILL NEED TO FINISH WHAT I STARTED?

NEW IDEAS, WISDOM, MINDSET SHIFTS:

_____

_____

_____

_____

_____

_____

_____

_____

_____

_____

_____

_____

_____

_____

_____

_____

_____

_____

THIS WEEK, I'M THANKFUL THAT I GET TO:

3 THINGS TO FINISH THIS WEEK:

MONDAY

PRIORITIES

TUESDAY

PRIORITIES

WEDNESDAY

PRIORITIES

FUEL TO FINISH: (PRAYERS, SCRIPTURE, MEMOS TO SELF...)

THURSDAY

PRIORITIES

_____
_____
_____
_____
_____

FRIDAY

PRIORITIES

_____
_____
_____
_____
_____

SATURDAY

SUNDAY

WEEKLY REFLECTION

HOW DID I FEEL ABOUT THIS WEEK?

ONE AMAZING THING THAT HAPPENED?

WHAT WILL I DO BETTER/DIFFERENTLY NEXT WEEK?

THINGS TO PRAY ABOUT (& NOT WORRY ABOUT)?

WHY DO I STILL NEED TO FINISH WHAT I STARTED?

NEW IDEAS, WISDOM, MINDSET SHIFTS:

_____

_____

_____

_____

_____

_____

_____

_____

_____

_____

_____

_____

_____

_____

_____

_____

_____

_____

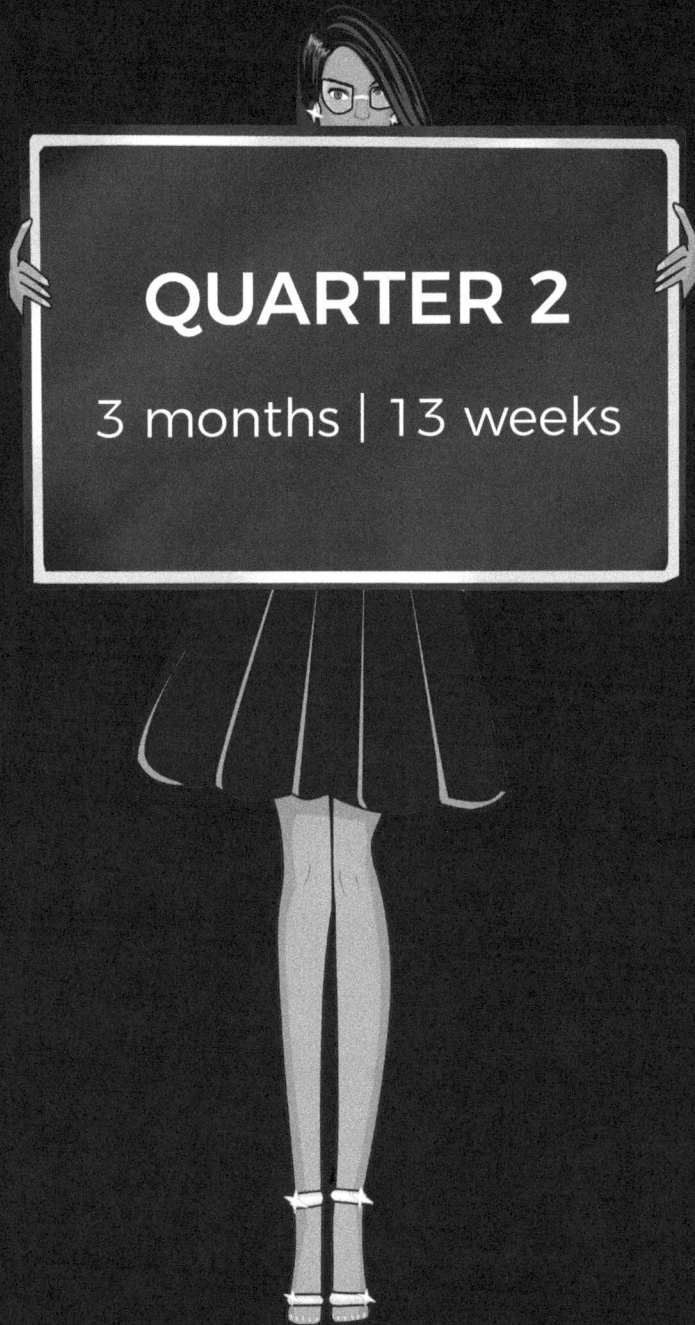

QUARTER 2

3 months | 13 weeks

QUARTER 2 - MY RESOLUTION TO FINISH

God has stirred my heart & asked me to create: (THE CALL)

So this quarter I will prioritize: (THE WHAT)

I need to finish this because: (THE WHY)

I cannot **make** time so I will **take** time from: (THE HOW)

I will set aside non-negotiable time to do this on: (THE WHEN)

To minimize distractions, I will go do this at: (THE WHERE)

To get accountability and snitch on my excuses, I will tell: (THE WHO)

Once this is done, I will finally feel: (THE WIN)

THIS QUARTER'S PROJECT:

I will complete _____

by _____

PROJECT DUMP: (LIST ALL POSSIBLE TASKS)

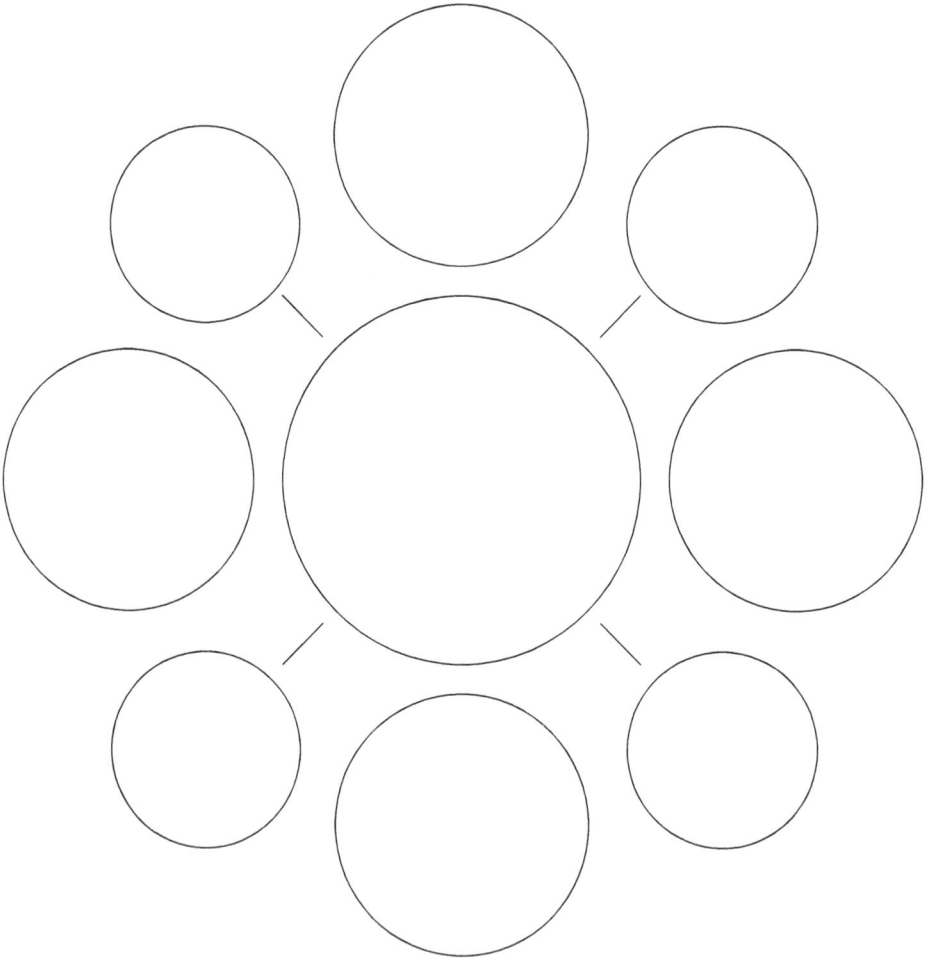

THIS QUARTER'S PRIORITIES

MONTH 1:

MONTH 2:

MONTH 3:

Month 1

1. _____

2. _____

3. _____

4. _____

5. _____

NOTES

_____

_____

_____

_____

_____

_____

_____

Call to me and I
will answer you,
and tell you great
and hidden things.

Jeremiah 33:3

SUNDAY	MONDAY	TUESDAY

WEDNESDAY	THURSDAY	FRIDAY	SATURDAY

THIS WEEK, I'M THANKFUL THAT I GET TO:

3 THINGS TO FINISH THIS WEEK:

MONDAY

PRIORITIES

TUESDAY

PRIORITIES

WEDNESDAY

PRIORITIES

FUEL TO FINISH: (PRAYERS, SCRIPTURE, MEMOS TO SELF...)

THURSDAY

PRIORITIES

FRIDAY

PRIORITIES

SATURDAY

SUNDAY

WEEKLY REFLECTION

HOW DID I FEEL ABOUT THIS WEEK?

ONE AMAZING THING THAT HAPPENED?

WHAT WILL I DO BETTER/DIFFERENTLY NEXT WEEK?

THINGS TO PRAY ABOUT (& NOT WORRY ABOUT)?

WHY DO I STILL NEED TO FINISH WHAT I STARTED?

NEW IDEAS, WISDOM, MINDSET SHIFTS:

THIS WEEK, I'M THANKFUL THAT I GET TO:

3 THINGS TO FINISH THIS WEEK:

MONDAY

PRIORITIES

TUESDAY

PRIORITIES

WEDNESDAY

PRIORITIES

FUEL TO FINISH: (PRAYERS, SCRIPTURE, MEMOS TO SELF...)

THURSDAY

PRIORITIES

FRIDAY

PRIORITIES

SATURDAY

SUNDAY

WEEKLY REFLECTION

HOW DID I FEEL ABOUT THIS WEEK?

ONE AMAZING THING THAT HAPPENED?

WHAT WILL I DO BETTER/DIFFERENTLY NEXT WEEK?

THINGS TO PRAY ABOUT (& NOT WORRY ABOUT)?

WHY DO I STILL NEED TO FINISH WHAT I STARTED?

NEW IDEAS, WISDOM, MINDSET SHIFTS:

_____

_____

_____

_____

_____

_____

_____

_____

_____

_____

_____

_____

_____

_____

_____

_____

_____

_____

THIS WEEK, I'M THANKFUL THAT I GET TO:

3 THINGS TO FINISH THIS WEEK:

MONDAY

PRIORITIES

TUESDAY

PRIORITIES

WEDNESDAY

PRIORITIES

FUEL TO FINISH: (PRAYERS, SCRIPTURE, MEMOS TO SELF...)

THURSDAY

PRIORITIES

FRIDAY

PRIORITIES

SATURDAY

SUNDAY

WEEKLY REFLECTION

HOW DID I FEEL ABOUT THIS WEEK?

ONE AMAZING THING THAT HAPPENED?

WHAT WILL I DO BETTER/DIFFERENTLY NEXT WEEK?

THINGS TO PRAY ABOUT (& NOT WORRY ABOUT)?

WHY DO I STILL NEED TO FINISH WHAT I STARTED?

NEW IDEAS, WISDOM, MINDSET SHIFTS:

_____

_____

_____

_____

_____

_____

_____

_____

_____

_____

_____

_____

_____

_____

_____

_____

_____

_____

_____

THIS WEEK, I'M THANKFUL THAT I GET TO:

3 THINGS TO FINISH THIS WEEK:

MONDAY

PRIORITIES

TUESDAY

PRIORITIES

WEDNESDAY

PRIORITIES

FUEL TO FINISH: (PRAYERS, SCRIPTURE, MEMOS TO SELF...)

THURSDAY

PRIORITIES

_____
_____
_____
_____
_____

FRIDAY

PRIORITIES

_____
_____
_____
_____
_____

SATURDAY

SUNDAY

WEEKLY REFLECTION

HOW DID I FEEL ABOUT THIS WEEK?

ONE AMAZING THING THAT HAPPENED?

WHAT WILL I DO BETTER/DIFFERENTLY NEXT WEEK?

THINGS TO PRAY ABOUT (& NOT WORRY ABOUT)?

WHY DO I STILL NEED TO FINISH WHAT I STARTED?

NEW IDEAS, WISDOM, MINDSET SHIFTS:

_____

_____

_____

_____

_____

_____

_____

_____

_____

_____

_____

_____

_____

_____

_____

_____

_____

_____

_____

1. _____

2. _____

3. _____

4. _____

5. _____

Month **2**

SUNDAY	MONDAY	TUESDAY

NOTES

_____

_____

_____

_____

_____

_____

_____

Whatever you do, work heartily, as for the Lord & not for men.

Colossians 3:23

WEDNESDAY	THURSDAY	FRIDAY	SATURDAY

THIS WEEK, I'M THANKFUL THAT I GET TO:

3 THINGS TO FINISH THIS WEEK:

MONDAY

PRIORITIES

TUESDAY

PRIORITIES

WEDNESDAY

PRIORITIES

FUEL TO FINISH: (PRAYERS, SCRIPTURE, MEMOS TO SELF...)

THURSDAY

PRIORITIES

_____
_____
_____
_____
_____

FRIDAY

PRIORITIES

_____
_____
_____
_____
_____

SATURDAY

SUNDAY

WEEKLY REFLECTION

HOW DID I FEEL ABOUT THIS WEEK?

ONE AMAZING THING THAT HAPPENED?

WHAT WILL I DO BETTER/DIFFERENTLY NEXT WEEK?

THINGS TO PRAY ABOUT (& NOT WORRY ABOUT)?

WHY DO I STILL NEED TO FINISH WHAT I STARTED?

NEW IDEAS, WISDOM, MINDSET SHIFTS:

_____

_____

_____

_____

_____

_____

_____

_____

_____

_____

_____

_____

_____

_____

_____

_____

_____

_____

_____

THIS WEEK, I'M THANKFUL THAT I GET TO:

3 THINGS TO FINISH THIS WEEK:

MONDAY

PRIORITIES

TUESDAY

PRIORITIES

WEDNESDAY

PRIORITIES

FUEL TO FINISH: (PRAYERS, SCRIPTURE, MEMOS TO SELF...)

THURSDAY

PRIORITIES

_____

_____

_____

_____

FRIDAY

PRIORITIES

_____

_____

_____

_____

SATURDAY

SUNDAY

WEEKLY REFLECTION

HOW DID I FEEL ABOUT THIS WEEK?

ONE AMAZING THING THAT HAPPENED?

WHAT WILL I DO BETTER/DIFFERENTLY NEXT WEEK?

THINGS TO PRAY ABOUT (& NOT WORRY ABOUT)?

WHY DO I STILL NEED TO FINISH WHAT I STARTED?

NEW IDEAS, WISDOM, MINDSET SHIFTS:

_____

_____

_____

_____

_____

_____

_____

_____

_____

_____

_____

_____

_____

_____

_____

_____

_____

_____

_____

THIS WEEK, I'M THANKFUL THAT I GET TO:

3 THINGS TO FINISH THIS WEEK:

MONDAY

PRIORITIES

TUESDAY

PRIORITIES

WEDNESDAY

PRIORITIES

FUEL TO FINISH: (PRAYERS, SCRIPTURE, MEMOS TO SELF...)

THURSDAY

PRIORITIES

_____
_____
_____
_____

FRIDAY

PRIORITIES

_____
_____
_____
_____

SATURDAY

SUNDAY

WEEKLY REFLECTION

HOW DID I FEEL ABOUT THIS WEEK?

ONE AMAZING THING THAT HAPPENED?

WHAT WILL I DO BETTER/DIFFERENTLY NEXT WEEK?

THINGS TO PRAY ABOUT (& NOT WORRY ABOUT)?

WHY DO I STILL NEED TO FINISH WHAT I STARTED?

NEW IDEAS, WISDOM, MINDSET SHIFTS:

_____

_____

_____

_____

_____

_____

_____

_____

_____

_____

_____

_____

_____

_____

_____

_____

_____

_____

THIS WEEK, I'M THANKFUL THAT I GET TO:

3 THINGS TO FINISH THIS WEEK:

MONDAY

PRIORITIES

TUESDAY

PRIORITIES

WEDNESDAY

PRIORITIES

FUEL TO FINISH: (PRAYERS, SCRIPTURE, MEMOS TO SELF...)

THURSDAY

PRIORITIES

_____
_____
_____
_____
_____

FRIDAY

PRIORITIES

_____
_____
_____
_____
_____

SATURDAY

SUNDAY

WEEKLY REFLECTION

HOW DID I FEEL ABOUT THIS WEEK?

ONE AMAZING THING THAT HAPPENED?

WHAT WILL I DO BETTER/DIFFERENTLY NEXT WEEK?

THINGS TO PRAY ABOUT (& NOT WORRY ABOUT)?

WHY DO I STILL NEED TO FINISH WHAT I STARTED?

NEW IDEAS, WISDOM, MINDSET SHIFTS:

_____

_____

_____

_____

_____

_____

_____

_____

_____

_____

_____

_____

_____

_____

_____

_____

_____

_____

THIS WEEK, I'M THANKFUL THAT I GET TO:

3 THINGS TO FINISH THIS WEEK:

MONDAY

PRIORITIES
_____
_____
_____
_____

TUESDAY

PRIORITIES
_____
_____
_____
_____
_____

WEDNESDAY

PRIORITIES
_____
_____
_____
_____

FUEL TO FINISH: (PRAYERS, SCRIPTURE, MEMOS TO SELF...)

THURSDAY

FRIDAY

SATURDAY

SUNDAY

WEEKLY REFLECTION

HOW DID I FEEL ABOUT THIS WEEK?

ONE AMAZING THING THAT HAPPENED?

WHAT WILL I DO BETTER/DIFFERENTLY NEXT WEEK?

THINGS TO PRAY ABOUT (& NOT WORRY ABOUT)?

WHY DO I STILL NEED TO FINISH WHAT I STARTED?

NEW IDEAS, WISDOM, MINDSET SHIFTS:

_____

_____

_____

_____

_____

_____

_____

_____

_____

_____

_____

_____

_____

_____

_____

_____

_____

_____

1. _____

2. _____

3. _____

4. _____

5. _____

NOTES

_____

_____

_____

_____

_____

_____

_____

Let perseverance
finish its work so
that you may be
mature & complete.

James 1:4

Month **3**

SUNDAY	MONDAY	TUESDAY

WEDNESDAY	THURSDAY	FRIDAY	SATURDAY

THIS WEEK, I'M THANKFUL THAT I GET TO:

3 THINGS TO FINISH THIS WEEK:

MONDAY

PRIORITIES

_____

_____

_____

_____

TUESDAY

PRIORITIES

_____

_____

_____

_____

_____

WEDNESDAY

PRIORITIES

_____

_____

_____

_____

FUEL TO FINISH: (PRAYERS, SCRIPTURE, MEMOS TO SELF...)

THURSDAY

PRIORITIES

_____
_____
_____
_____
_____

FRIDAY

PRIORITIES

_____
_____
_____
_____
_____

SATURDAY

SUNDAY

WEEKLY REFLECTION

HOW DID I FEEL ABOUT THIS WEEK?

ONE AMAZING THING THAT HAPPENED?

WHAT WILL I DO BETTER/DIFFERENTLY NEXT WEEK?

THINGS TO PRAY ABOUT (& NOT WORRY ABOUT)?

WHY DO I STILL NEED TO FINISH WHAT I STARTED?

NEW IDEAS, WISDOM, MINDSET SHIFTS:

_____

_____

_____

_____

_____

_____

_____

_____

_____

_____

_____

_____

_____

_____

_____

_____

_____

_____

THIS WEEK, I'M THANKFUL THAT I GET TO:

3 THINGS TO FINISH THIS WEEK:

MONDAY

PRIORITIES

TUESDAY

PRIORITIES

WEDNESDAY

PRIORITIES

FUEL TO FINISH: (PRAYERS, SCRIPTURE, MEMOS TO SELF...)

THURSDAY

FRIDAY

SATURDAY

SUNDAY

WEEKLY REFLECTION

HOW DID I FEEL ABOUT THIS WEEK?

ONE AMAZING THING THAT HAPPENED?

WHAT WILL I DO BETTER/DIFFERENTLY NEXT WEEK?

THINGS TO PRAY ABOUT (& NOT WORRY ABOUT)?

WHY DO I STILL NEED TO FINISH WHAT I STARTED?

NEW IDEAS, WISDOM, MINDSET SHIFTS:

_____

_____

_____

_____

_____

_____

_____

_____

_____

_____

_____

_____

_____

_____

_____

_____

_____

_____

_____

THIS WEEK, I'M THANKFUL THAT I GET TO:

3 THINGS TO FINISH THIS WEEK:

MONDAY

PRIORITIES

_____

_____

_____

_____

TUESDAY

PRIORITIES

_____

_____

_____

_____

WEDNESDAY

PRIORITIES

_____

_____

_____

_____

FUEL TO FINISH: (PRAYERS, SCRIPTURE, MEMOS TO SELF...)

THURSDAY

PRIORITIES

FRIDAY

PRIORITIES

SATURDAY

SUNDAY

WEEKLY REFLECTION

HOW DID I FEEL ABOUT THIS WEEK?

ONE AMAZING THING THAT HAPPENED?

WHAT WILL I DO BETTER/DIFFERENTLY NEXT WEEK?

THINGS TO PRAY ABOUT (& NOT WORRY ABOUT)?

WHY DO I STILL NEED TO FINISH WHAT I STARTED?

NEW IDEAS, WISDOM, MINDSET SHIFTS:

THIS WEEK, I'M THANKFUL THAT I GET TO:

3 THINGS TO FINISH THIS WEEK:

MONDAY

PRIORITIES

TUESDAY

PRIORITIES

WEDNESDAY

PRIORITIES

FUEL TO FINISH: (PRAYERS, SCRIPTURE, MEMOS TO SELF...)

THURSDAY

PRIORITIES

_____
_____
_____
_____

FRIDAY

PRIORITIES

_____
_____
_____
_____

SATURDAY

SUNDAY

WEEKLY REFLECTION

HOW DID I FEEL ABOUT THIS WEEK?

ONE AMAZING THING THAT HAPPENED?

WHAT WILL I DO BETTER/DIFFERENTLY NEXT WEEK?

THINGS TO PRAY ABOUT (& NOT WORRY ABOUT)?

WHY DO I STILL NEED TO FINISH WHAT I STARTED?

NEW IDEAS, WISDOM, MINDSET SHIFTS:

QUARTER 3
3 months | 13 weeks

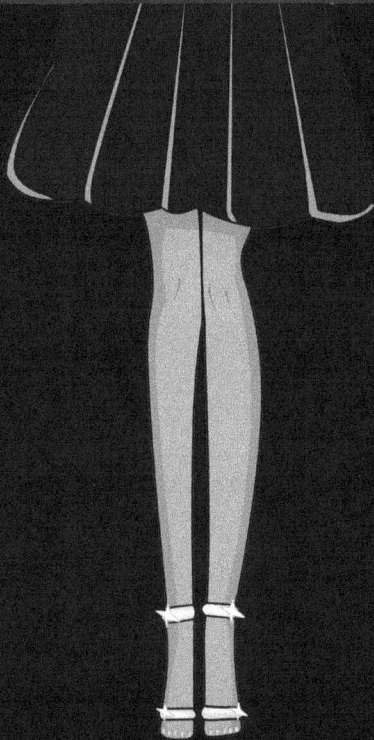

QUARTER 3 - MY RESOLUTION TO FINISH

God has stirred my heart & asked me to create: (THE CALL)

So this quarter I will prioritize: (THE WHAT)

I need to finish this because: (THE WHY)

I cannot **make** time so I will **take** time from: (THE HOW)

I will set aside non-negotiable time to do this on: (THE WHEN)

To minimize distractions, I will go do this at: (THE WHERE)

To get accountability and snitch on my excuses, I will tell: (THE WHO)

Once this is done, I will finally feel: (THE WIN)

THIS QUARTER'S PROJECT:

I will complete _____

by _____

PROJECT DUMP: (LIST ALL POSSIBLE TASKS)

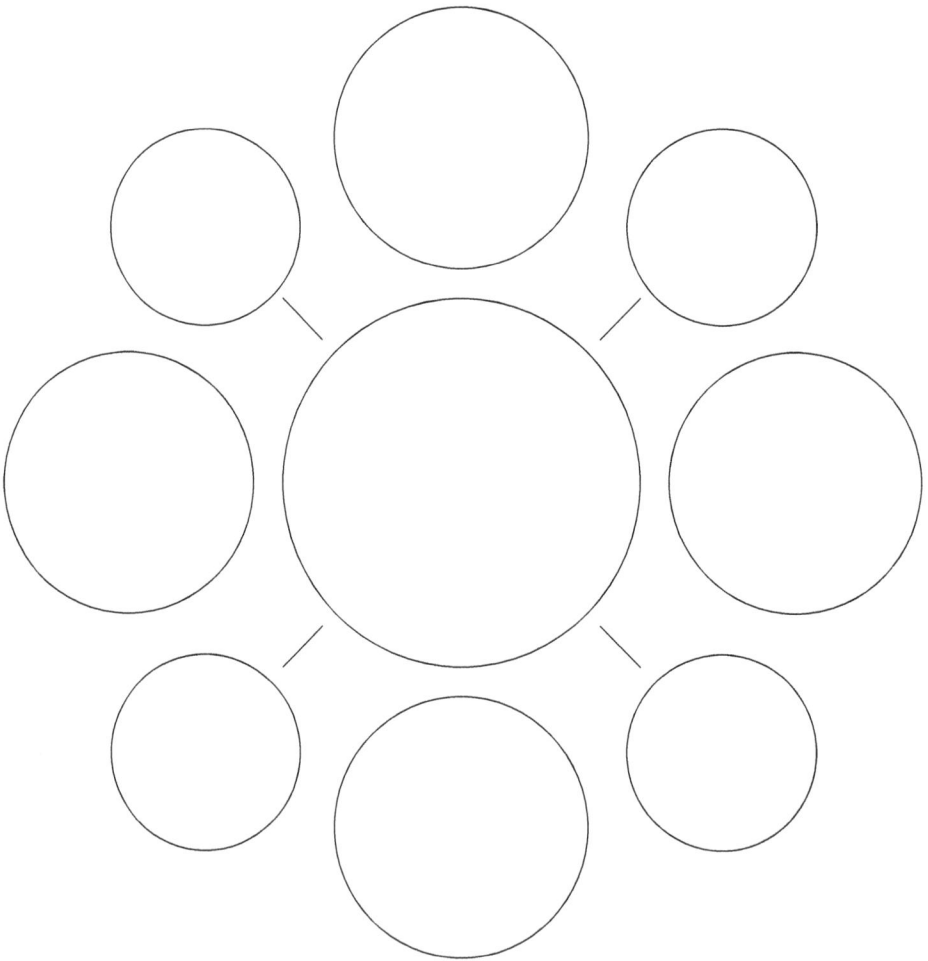

THIS QUARTER'S PRIORITIES

(ASSIGN ESSENTIAL TASKS TO A SPECIFIC MONTH)

MONTH 1:

MONTH 2:

MONTH 3:

Month **1**

1. _____

2. _____

3. _____

4. _____

5. _____

NOTES

_____

_____

_____

_____

_____

_____

_____

So we say with
confidence, "The
Lord is my helper; I
will not be afraid."

Hebrews 13:6

SUNDAY	MONDAY	TUESDAY

WEDNESDAY	THURSDAY	FRIDAY	SATURDAY

THIS WEEK, I'M THANKFUL THAT I GET TO:

3 THINGS TO FINISH THIS WEEK:

MONDAY

PRIORITIES

_____
_____
_____
_____

TUESDAY

PRIORITIES

_____
_____
_____
_____

WEDNESDAY

PRIORITIES

_____
_____
_____
_____

FUEL TO FINISH: (PRAYERS, SCRIPTURE, MEMOS TO SELF...)

THURSDAY

PRIORITIES

FRIDAY

PRIORITIES

SATURDAY

SUNDAY

WEEKLY REFLECTION

HOW DID I FEEL ABOUT THIS WEEK?

ONE AMAZING THING THAT HAPPENED?

WHAT WILL I DO BETTER/DIFFERENTLY NEXT WEEK?

THINGS TO PRAY ABOUT (& NOT WORRY ABOUT)?

WHY DO I STILL NEED TO FINISH WHAT I STARTED?

NEW IDEAS, WISDOM, MINDSET SHIFTS:

THIS WEEK, I'M THANKFUL THAT I GET TO:

3 THINGS TO FINISH THIS WEEK:

MONDAY

PRIORITIES

_____

_____

_____

_____

TUESDAY

PRIORITIES

_____

_____

_____

_____

WEDNESDAY

PRIORITIES

_____

_____

_____

_____

FUEL TO FINISH: (PRAYERS, SCRIPTURE, MEMOS TO SELF...)

THURSDAY

PRIORITIES

_____

_____

_____

_____

_____

FRIDAY

PRIORITIES

_____

_____

_____

_____

_____

SATURDAY

SUNDAY

WEEKLY REFLECTION

HOW DID I FEEL ABOUT THIS WEEK?

ONE AMAZING THING THAT HAPPENED?

WHAT WILL I DO BETTER/DIFFERENTLY NEXT WEEK?

THINGS TO PRAY ABOUT (& NOT WORRY ABOUT)?

WHY DO I STILL NEED TO FINISH WHAT I STARTED?

NEW IDEAS, WISDOM, MINDSET SHIFTS:

THIS WEEK, I'M THANKFUL THAT I GET TO:

3 THINGS TO FINISH THIS WEEK:

MONDAY

PRIORITIES

TUESDAY

PRIORITIES

WEDNESDAY

PRIORITIES

FUEL TO FINISH: (PRAYERS, SCRIPTURE, MEMOS TO SELF...)

THURSDAY

PRIORITIES

_____

_____

_____

_____

FRIDAY

PRIORITIES

_____

_____

_____

_____

SATURDAY

SUNDAY

WEEKLY REFLECTION

HOW DID I FEEL ABOUT THIS WEEK?

ONE AMAZING THING THAT HAPPENED?

WHAT WILL I DO BETTER/DIFFERENTLY NEXT WEEK?

THINGS TO PRAY ABOUT (& NOT WORRY ABOUT)?

WHY DO I STILL NEED TO FINISH WHAT I STARTED?

NEW IDEAS, WISDOM, MINDSET SHIFTS:

_____

_____

_____

_____

_____

_____

_____

_____

_____

_____

_____

_____

_____

_____

_____

_____

_____

_____

THIS WEEK, I'M THANKFUL THAT I GET TO:

3 THINGS TO FINISH THIS WEEK:

MONDAY

PRIORITIES

_____
_____
_____
_____

TUESDAY

PRIORITIES

_____
_____
_____
_____

WEDNESDAY

PRIORITIES

_____
_____
_____
_____

FUEL TO FINISH: (PRAYERS, SCRIPTURE, MEMOS TO SELF...)

THURSDAY

PRIORITIES

FRIDAY

PRIORITIES

SATURDAY

SUNDAY

WEEKLY REFLECTION

HOW DID I FEEL ABOUT THIS WEEK?

ONE AMAZING THING THAT HAPPENED?

WHAT WILL I DO BETTER/DIFFERENTLY NEXT WEEK?

THINGS TO PRAY ABOUT (& NOT WORRY ABOUT)?

WHY DO I STILL NEED TO FINISH WHAT I STARTED?

NEW IDEAS, WISDOM, MINDSET SHIFTS:

_____

_____

_____

_____

_____

_____

_____

_____

_____

_____

_____

_____

_____

_____

_____

_____

_____

_____

Month **2**

1. _____

2. _____

3. _____

4. _____

5. _____

NOTES

_____

_____

_____

_____

_____

_____

_____

Teach us to
number our days
that we may gain
a heart of wisdom.

Psalm 90:12

SUNDAY	MONDAY	TUESDAY

WEDNESDAY	THURSDAY	FRIDAY	SATURDAY

THIS WEEK, I'M THANKFUL THAT I GET TO:

3 THINGS TO FINISH THIS WEEK:

MONDAY

PRIORITIES

TUESDAY

PRIORITIES

WEDNESDAY

PRIORITIES

FUEL TO FINISH: (PRAYERS, SCRIPTURE, MEMOS TO SELF...)

THURSDAY

PRIORITIES

FRIDAY

PRIORITIES

SATURDAY

SUNDAY

WEEKLY REFLECTION

HOW DID I FEEL ABOUT THIS WEEK?

ONE AMAZING THING THAT HAPPENED?

WHAT WILL I DO BETTER/DIFFERENTLY NEXT WEEK?

THINGS TO PRAY ABOUT (& NOT WORRY ABOUT)?

WHY DO I STILL NEED TO FINISH WHAT I STARTED?

NEW IDEAS, WISDOM, MINDSET SHIFTS:

THIS WEEK, I'M THANKFUL THAT I GET TO:

3 THINGS TO FINISH THIS WEEK:

MONDAY

PRIORITIES

TUESDAY

PRIORITIES

WEDNESDAY

PRIORITIES

FUEL TO FINISH: (PRAYERS, SCRIPTURE, MEMOS TO SELF...)

THURSDAY

PRIORITIES

FRIDAY

PRIORITIES

SATURDAY

SUNDAY

WEEKLY REFLECTION

HOW DID I FEEL ABOUT THIS WEEK?

ONE AMAZING THING THAT HAPPENED?

WHAT WILL I DO BETTER/DIFFERENTLY NEXT WEEK?

THINGS TO PRAY ABOUT (& NOT WORRY ABOUT)?

WHY DO I STILL NEED TO FINISH WHAT I STARTED?

NEW IDEAS, WISDOM, MINDSET SHIFTS:

_____

_____

_____

_____

_____

_____

_____

_____

_____

_____

_____

_____

_____

_____

_____

_____

_____

_____

THIS WEEK, I'M THANKFUL THAT I GET TO:

3 THINGS TO FINISH THIS WEEK:

MONDAY

PRIORITIES

_____
_____
_____
_____

TUESDAY

PRIORITIES

_____
_____
_____
_____

WEDNESDAY

PRIORITIES

_____
_____
_____
_____

FUEL TO FINISH: (PRAYERS, SCRIPTURE, MEMOS TO SELF...)

THURSDAY

PRIORITIES

_____
_____
_____
_____
_____

FRIDAY

PRIORITIES

_____
_____
_____
_____
_____

SATURDAY

SUNDAY

WEEKLY REFLECTION

HOW DID I FEEL ABOUT THIS WEEK?

ONE AMAZING THING THAT HAPPENED?

WHAT WILL I DO BETTER/DIFFERENTLY NEXT WEEK?

THINGS TO PRAY ABOUT (& NOT WORRY ABOUT)?

WHY DO I STILL NEED TO FINISH WHAT I STARTED?

NEW IDEAS, WISDOM, MINDSET SHIFTS:

_____

_____

_____

_____

_____

_____

_____

_____

_____

_____

_____

_____

_____

_____

_____

_____

_____

_____

THIS WEEK, I'M THANKFUL THAT I GET TO:

3 THINGS TO FINISH THIS WEEK:

MONDAY

PRIORITIES

_____
_____
_____
_____

TUESDAY

PRIORITIES

_____
_____
_____
_____

WEDNESDAY

PRIORITIES

_____
_____
_____
_____

FUEL TO FINISH: (PRAYERS, SCRIPTURE, MEMOS TO SELF...)

THURSDAY

PRIORITIES

_____

_____

_____

_____

_____

FRIDAY

PRIORITIES

_____

_____

_____

_____

_____

SATURDAY

SUNDAY

WEEKLY REFLECTION

HOW DID I FEEL ABOUT THIS WEEK?

ONE AMAZING THING THAT HAPPENED?

WHAT WILL I DO BETTER/DIFFERENTLY NEXT WEEK?

THINGS TO PRAY ABOUT (& NOT WORRY ABOUT)?

WHY DO I STILL NEED TO FINISH WHAT I STARTED?

NEW IDEAS, WISDOM, MINDSET SHIFTS:

_____

_____

_____

_____

_____

_____

_____

_____

_____

_____

_____

_____

_____

_____

_____

_____

_____

_____

_____

THIS WEEK, I'M THANKFUL THAT I GET TO:

3 THINGS TO FINISH THIS WEEK:

MONDAY

PRIORITIES

_____
_____
_____
_____

TUESDAY

PRIORITIES

_____
_____
_____
_____
_____

WEDNESDAY

PRIORITIES

_____
_____
_____
_____

FUEL TO FINISH: (PRAYERS, SCRIPTURE, MEMOS TO SELF...)

THURSDAY

PRIORITIES

FRIDAY

PRIORITIES

SATURDAY

SUNDAY

WEEKLY REFLECTION

HOW DID I FEEL ABOUT THIS WEEK?

ONE AMAZING THING THAT HAPPENED?

WHAT WILL I DO BETTER/DIFFERENTLY NEXT WEEK?

THINGS TO PRAY ABOUT (& NOT WORRY ABOUT)?

WHY DO I STILL NEED TO FINISH WHAT I STARTED?

NEW IDEAS, WISDOM, MINDSET SHIFTS:

_____

_____

_____

_____

_____

_____

_____

_____

_____

_____

_____

_____

_____

_____

_____

_____

_____

_____

_____

ITEMS TO FINISH FIRST:

1. _____

2. _____

3. _____

4. _____

5. _____

NOTES

_____

_____

_____

_____

_____

_____

_____

_____

"For I know the plans I have for you," declares the Lord.

Jeremiah 29:11

Month **3**

SUNDAY	MONDAY	TUESDAY

WEDNESDAY	THURSDAY	FRIDAY	SATURDAY

THIS WEEK, I'M THANKFUL THAT I GET TO:

3 THINGS TO FINISH THIS WEEK:

MONDAY

PRIORITIES

TUESDAY

PRIORITIES

WEDNESDAY

PRIORITIES

FUEL TO FINISH: (PRAYERS, SCRIPTURE, MEMOS TO SELF...)

THURSDAY

PRIORITIES

_____
_____
_____
_____
_____

FRIDAY

PRIORITIES

_____
_____
_____
_____
_____

SATURDAY

SUNDAY

WEEKLY REFLECTION

HOW DID I FEEL ABOUT THIS WEEK?

ONE AMAZING THING THAT HAPPENED?

WHAT WILL I DO BETTER/DIFFERENTLY NEXT WEEK?

THINGS TO PRAY ABOUT (& NOT WORRY ABOUT)?

WHY DO I STILL NEED TO FINISH WHAT I STARTED?

NEW IDEAS, WISDOM, MINDSET SHIFTS:

_____

_____

_____

_____

_____

_____

_____

_____

_____

_____

_____

_____

_____

_____

_____

_____

_____

_____

THIS WEEK, I'M THANKFUL THAT I GET TO:

3 THINGS TO FINISH THIS WEEK:

MONDAY

PRIORITIES

TUESDAY

PRIORITIES

WEDNESDAY

PRIORITIES

FUEL TO FINISH: (PRAYERS, SCRIPTURE, MEMOS TO SELF...)

THURSDAY

PRIORITIES

FRIDAY

PRIORITIES

SATURDAY

SUNDAY

WEEKLY REFLECTION

HOW DID I FEEL ABOUT THIS WEEK?

ONE AMAZING THING THAT HAPPENED?

WHAT WILL I DO BETTER/DIFFERENTLY NEXT WEEK?

THINGS TO PRAY ABOUT (& NOT WORRY ABOUT)?

WHY DO I STILL NEED TO FINISH WHAT I STARTED?

NEW IDEAS, WISDOM, MINDSET SHIFTS:

THIS WEEK, I'M THANKFUL THAT I GET TO:

3 THINGS TO FINISH THIS WEEK:

MONDAY

PRIORITIES

TUESDAY

PRIORITIES

WEDNESDAY

PRIORITIES

FUEL TO FINISH: (PRAYERS, SCRIPTURE, MEMOS TO SELF...)

THURSDAY

PRIORITIES

FRIDAY

PRIORITIES

SATURDAY

SUNDAY

WEEKLY REFLECTION

HOW DID I FEEL ABOUT THIS WEEK?

ONE AMAZING THING THAT HAPPENED?

WHAT WILL I DO BETTER/DIFFERENTLY NEXT WEEK?

THINGS TO PRAY ABOUT (& NOT WORRY ABOUT)?

WHY DO I STILL NEED TO FINISH WHAT I STARTED?

NEW IDEAS, WISDOM, MINDSET SHIFTS:

THIS WEEK, I'M THANKFUL THAT I GET TO:

3 THINGS TO FINISH THIS WEEK:

MONDAY

PRIORITIES

_____
_____
_____
_____

TUESDAY

PRIORITIES

_____
_____
_____
_____
_____

WEDNESDAY

PRIORITIES

_____
_____
_____
_____

FUEL TO FINISH: (PRAYERS, SCRIPTURE, MEMOS TO SELF...)

THURSDAY

PRIORITIES

_____
_____
_____
_____
_____

FRIDAY

PRIORITIES

_____
_____
_____
_____
_____

SATURDAY

SUNDAY

WEEKLY REFLECTION

HOW DID I FEEL ABOUT THIS WEEK?

ONE AMAZING THING THAT HAPPENED?

WHAT WILL I DO BETTER/DIFFERENTLY NEXT WEEK?

THINGS TO PRAY ABOUT (& NOT WORRY ABOUT)?

WHY DO I STILL NEED TO FINISH WHAT I STARTED?

NEW IDEAS, WISDOM, MINDSET SHIFTS:

_____

_____

_____

_____

_____

_____

_____

_____

_____

_____

_____

_____

_____

_____

_____

_____

_____

_____

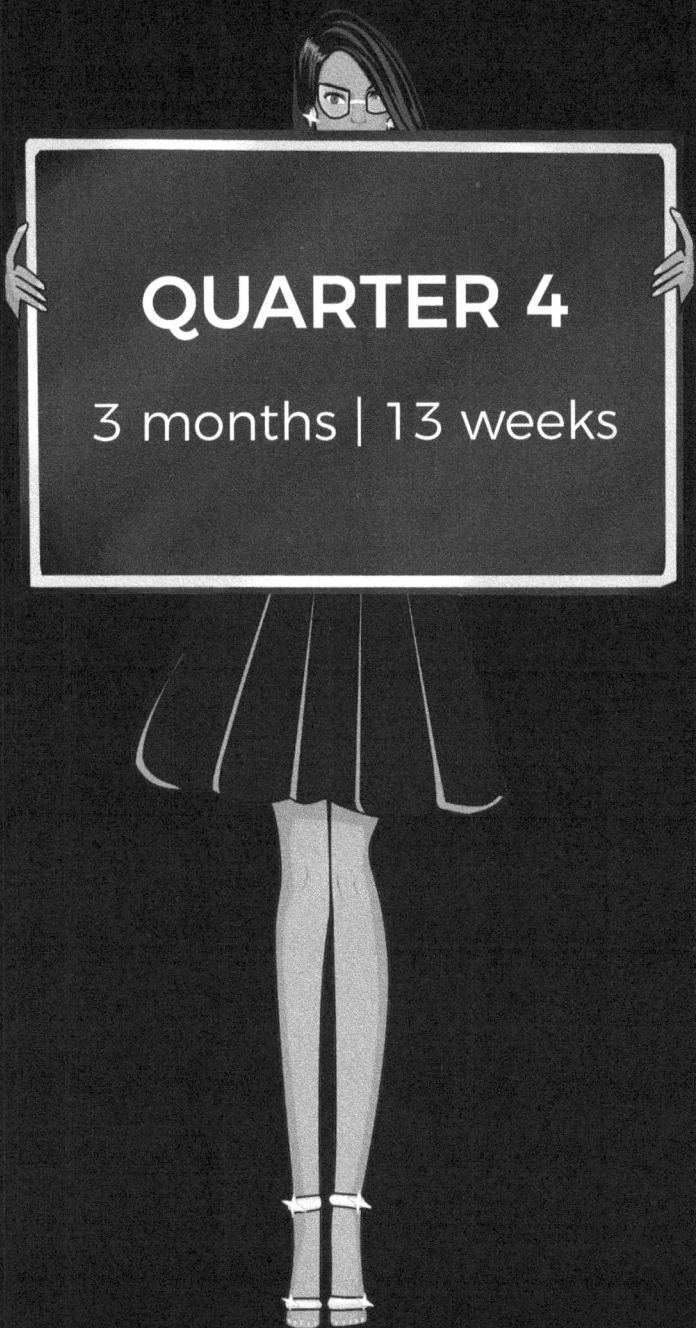

QUARTER 4

3 months | 13 weeks

QUARTER 4 - MY RESOLUTION TO FINISH

God has stirred my heart & asked me to create: (THE CALL)

So this quarter I will prioritize: (THE WHAT)

I need to finish this because: (THE WHY)

I cannot **make** time so I will **take** time from: (THE HOW)

I will set aside non-negotiable time to do this on: (THE WHEN)

To minimize distractions, I will go do this at: (THE WHERE)

To get accountability and snitch on my excuses, I will tell: (THE WHO)

Once this is done, I will finally feel: (THE WIN)

THIS QUARTER'S PROJECT:

I will complete _____

by _____

PROJECT DUMP: (LIST ALL POSSIBLE TASKS)

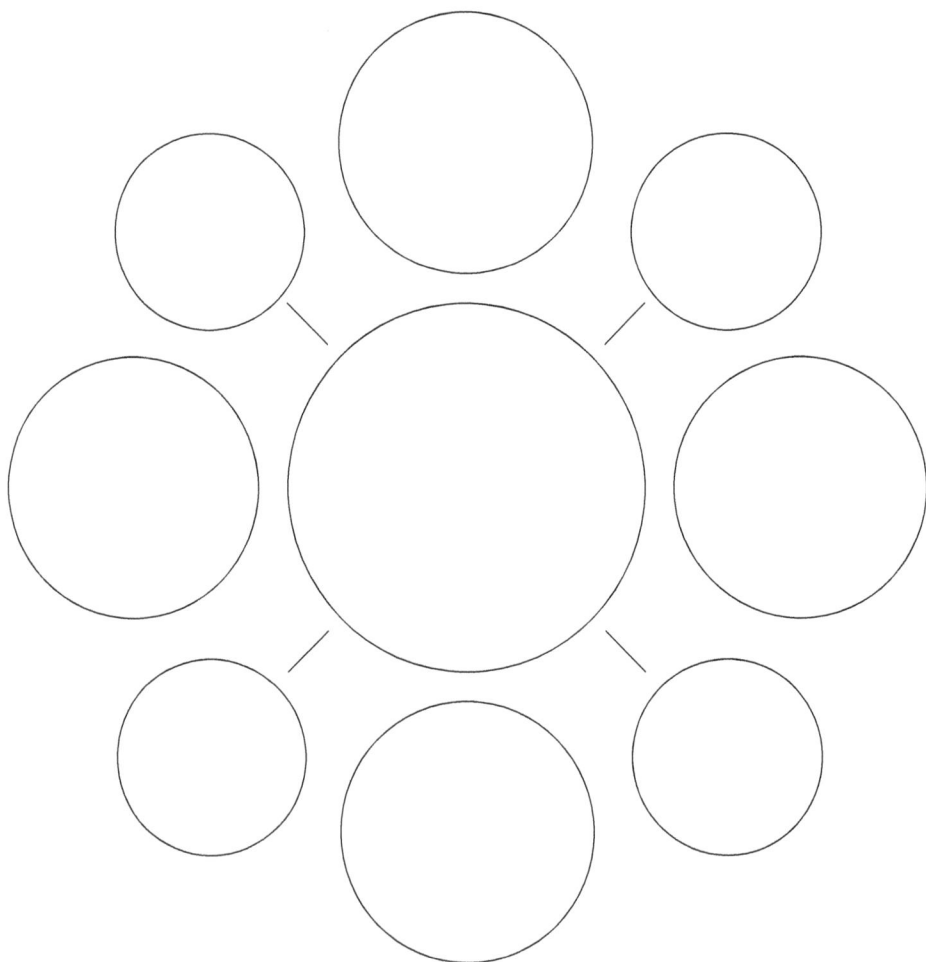

THIS QUARTER'S PRIORITIES

(ASSIGN ESSENTIAL TASKS TO A SPECIFIC MONTH)

MONTH 1:

MONTH 2:

MONTH 3:

Month **1**

1. _____

2. _____

3. _____

4. _____

5. _____

NOTES

_____

_____

_____

_____

_____

_____

_____

Unless the Lord
builds the house,
those who build it
labor in vain.

Psalm 127:1

SUNDAY	MONDAY	TUESDAY

WEDNESDAY	THURSDAY	FRIDAY	SATURDAY

THIS WEEK, I'M THANKFUL THAT I GET TO:

3 THINGS TO FINISH THIS WEEK:

MONDAY

PRIORITIES

_____

_____

_____

_____

TUESDAY

PRIORITIES

_____

_____

_____

_____

WEDNESDAY

PRIORITIES

_____

_____

_____

_____

FUEL TO FINISH: (PRAYERS, SCRIPTURE, MEMOS TO SELF...)

THURSDAY

PRIORITIES

_____
_____
_____
_____
_____

FRIDAY

PRIORITIES

_____
_____
_____
_____
_____

SATURDAY

SUNDAY

WEEKLY REFLECTION

HOW DID I FEEL ABOUT THIS WEEK?

ONE AMAZING THING THAT HAPPENED?

WHAT WILL I DO BETTER/DIFFERENTLY NEXT WEEK?

THINGS TO PRAY ABOUT (& NOT WORRY ABOUT)?

WHY DO I STILL NEED TO FINISH WHAT I STARTED?

NEW IDEAS, WISDOM, MINDSET SHIFTS:

THIS WEEK, I'M THANKFUL THAT I GET TO:

3 THINGS TO FINISH THIS WEEK:

MONDAY

PRIORITIES

TUESDAY

PRIORITIES

WEDNESDAY

PRIORITIES

FUEL TO FINISH: (PRAYERS, SCRIPTURE, MEMOS TO SELF...)

THURSDAY

PRIORITIES

FRIDAY

PRIORITIES

SATURDAY

SUNDAY

WEEKLY REFLECTION

HOW DID I FEEL ABOUT THIS WEEK?

ONE AMAZING THING THAT HAPPENED?

WHAT WILL I DO BETTER/DIFFERENTLY NEXT WEEK?

THINGS TO PRAY ABOUT (& NOT WORRY ABOUT)?

WHY DO I STILL NEED TO FINISH WHAT I STARTED?

NEW IDEAS, WISDOM, MINDSET SHIFTS:

THIS WEEK, I'M THANKFUL THAT I GET TO:

3 THINGS TO FINISH THIS WEEK:

MONDAY

PRIORITIES

TUESDAY

PRIORITIES

WEDNESDAY

PRIORITIES

FUEL TO FINISH: (PRAYERS, SCRIPTURE, MEMOS TO SELF...)

THURSDAY

PRIORITIES

_____
_____
_____
_____

FRIDAY

PRIORITIES

_____
_____
_____
_____

SATURDAY

SUNDAY

WEEKLY REFLECTION

HOW DID I FEEL ABOUT THIS WEEK?

ONE AMAZING THING THAT HAPPENED?

WHAT WILL I DO BETTER/DIFFERENTLY NEXT WEEK?

THINGS TO PRAY ABOUT (& NOT WORRY ABOUT)?

WHY DO I STILL NEED TO FINISH WHAT I STARTED?

NEW IDEAS, WISDOM, MINDSET SHIFTS:

THIS WEEK, I'M THANKFUL THAT I GET TO:

3 THINGS TO FINISH THIS WEEK:

MONDAY

PRIORITIES

_____

_____

_____

_____

TUESDAY

PRIORITIES

_____

_____

_____

_____

_____

WEDNESDAY

PRIORITIES

_____

_____

_____

_____

FUEL TO FINISH: (PRAYERS, SCRIPTURE, MEMOS TO SELF...)

THURSDAY

PRIORITIES

FRIDAY

PRIORITIES

SATURDAY

SUNDAY

WEEKLY REFLECTION

HOW DID I FEEL ABOUT THIS WEEK?

ONE AMAZING THING THAT HAPPENED?

WHAT WILL I DO BETTER/DIFFERENTLY NEXT WEEK?

THINGS TO PRAY ABOUT (& NOT WORRY ABOUT)?

WHY DO I STILL NEED TO FINISH WHAT I STARTED?

NEW IDEAS, WISDOM, MINDSET SHIFTS:

Month **2**

1. _____

2. _____

3. _____

4. _____

5. _____

NOTES

_____

_____

_____

_____

_____

_____

_____

But Jesus said,
"What is impossible
with man is
possible with God.

Luke 18:27

SUNDAY	MONDAY	TUESDAY

WEDNESDAY	THURSDAY	FRIDAY	SATURDAY

THIS WEEK, I'M THANKFUL THAT I GET TO:

3 THINGS TO FINISH THIS WEEK:

MONDAY

PRIORITIES

TUESDAY

PRIORITIES

WEDNESDAY

PRIORITIES

FUEL TO FINISH: (PRAYERS, SCRIPTURE, MEMOS TO SELF...)

THURSDAY

PRIORITIES

_____
_____
_____
_____

FRIDAY

PRIORITIES

_____
_____
_____
_____

SATURDAY

SUNDAY

WEEKLY REFLECTION

HOW DID I FEEL ABOUT THIS WEEK?

ONE AMAZING THING THAT HAPPENED?

WHAT WILL I DO BETTER/DIFFERENTLY NEXT WEEK?

THINGS TO PRAY ABOUT (& NOT WORRY ABOUT)?

WHY DO I STILL NEED TO FINISH WHAT I STARTED?

NEW IDEAS, WISDOM, MINDSET SHIFTS:

THIS WEEK, I'M THANKFUL THAT I GET TO:

3 THINGS TO FINISH THIS WEEK:

MONDAY

PRIORITIES

TUESDAY

PRIORITIES

WEDNESDAY

PRIORITIES

FUEL TO FINISH: (PRAYERS, SCRIPTURE, MEMOS TO SELF...)

THURSDAY

PRIORITIES

FRIDAY

PRIORITIES

SATURDAY

SUNDAY

WEEKLY REFLECTION

HOW DID I FEEL ABOUT THIS WEEK?

ONE AMAZING THING THAT HAPPENED?

WHAT WILL I DO BETTER/DIFFERENTLY NEXT WEEK?

THINGS TO PRAY ABOUT (& NOT WORRY ABOUT)?

WHY DO I STILL NEED TO FINISH WHAT I STARTED?

NEW IDEAS, WISDOM, MINDSET SHIFTS:

_____

_____

_____

_____

_____

_____

_____

_____

_____

_____

_____

_____

_____

_____

_____

_____

_____

_____

THIS WEEK, I'M THANKFUL THAT I GET TO:

3 THINGS TO FINISH THIS WEEK:

MONDAY

PRIORITIES

TUESDAY

PRIORITIES

WEDNESDAY

PRIORITIES

FUEL TO FINISH: (PRAYERS, SCRIPTURE, MEMOS TO SELF...)

THURSDAY

PRIORITIES

_____
_____
_____
_____

FRIDAY

PRIORITIES

_____
_____
_____
_____

SATURDAY

SUNDAY

WEEKLY REFLECTION

HOW DID I FEEL ABOUT THIS WEEK?

ONE AMAZING THING THAT HAPPENED?

WHAT WILL I DO BETTER/DIFFERENTLY NEXT WEEK?

THINGS TO PRAY ABOUT (& NOT WORRY ABOUT)?

WHY DO I STILL NEED TO FINISH WHAT I STARTED?

NEW IDEAS, WISDOM, MINDSET SHIFTS:

_____

_____

_____

_____

_____

_____

_____

_____

_____

_____

_____

_____

_____

_____

_____

_____

_____

_____

THIS WEEK, I'M THANKFUL THAT I GET TO:

3 THINGS TO FINISH THIS WEEK:

MONDAY

PRIORITIES

_____

_____

_____

_____

TUESDAY

PRIORITIES

_____

_____

_____

_____

_____

WEDNESDAY

PRIORITIES

_____

_____

_____

_____

FUEL TO FINISH: (PRAYERS, SCRIPTURE, MEMOS TO SELF...)

THURSDAY

PRIORITIES

_____
_____
_____
_____
_____

FRIDAY

PRIORITIES

_____
_____
_____
_____
_____

SATURDAY

SUNDAY

WEEKLY REFLECTION

HOW DID I FEEL ABOUT THIS WEEK?

ONE AMAZING THING THAT HAPPENED?

WHAT WILL I DO BETTER/DIFFERENTLY NEXT WEEK?

THINGS TO PRAY ABOUT (& NOT WORRY ABOUT)?

WHY DO I STILL NEED TO FINISH WHAT I STARTED?

NEW IDEAS, WISDOM, MINDSET SHIFTS:

_____

_____

_____

_____

_____

_____

_____

_____

_____

_____

_____

_____

_____

_____

_____

_____

_____

_____

THIS WEEK, I'M THANKFUL THAT I GET TO:

3 THINGS TO FINISH THIS WEEK:

MONDAY

PRIORITIES

TUESDAY

PRIORITIES

WEDNESDAY

PRIORITIES

FUEL TO FINISH: (PRAYERS, SCRIPTURE, MEMOS TO SELF...)

THURSDAY

PRIORITIES

_____
_____
_____
_____
_____

FRIDAY

PRIORITIES

_____
_____
_____
_____
_____

SATURDAY

SUNDAY

WEEKLY REFLECTION

HOW DID I FEEL ABOUT THIS WEEK?

ONE AMAZING THING THAT HAPPENED?

WHAT WILL I DO BETTER/DIFFERENTLY NEXT WEEK?

THINGS TO PRAY ABOUT (& NOT WORRY ABOUT)?

WHY DO I STILL NEED TO FINISH WHAT I STARTED?

NEW IDEAS, WISDOM, MINDSET SHIFTS:

_____

_____

_____

_____

_____

_____

_____

_____

_____

_____

_____

_____

_____

_____

_____

_____

_____

1. _____

2. _____

3. _____

4. _____

5. _____

Month **3**

SUNDAY	MONDAY	TUESDAY

NOTES

_____

_____

_____

_____

_____

_____

_____

For you need
endurance to do
God's will and
receive what is
promised.

Hebrews 10:36

WEDNESDAY	THURSDAY	FRIDAY	SATURDAY

THIS WEEK, I'M THANKFUL THAT I GET TO:

3 THINGS TO FINISH THIS WEEK:

MONDAY

PRIORITIES

TUESDAY

PRIORITIES

WEDNESDAY

PRIORITIES

FUEL TO FINISH: (PRAYERS, SCRIPTURE, MEMOS TO SELF...)

THURSDAY

PRIORITIES

FRIDAY

PRIORITIES

SATURDAY

SUNDAY

WEEKLY REFLECTION

HOW DID I FEEL ABOUT THIS WEEK?

ONE AMAZING THING THAT HAPPENED?

WHAT WILL I DO BETTER/DIFFERENTLY NEXT WEEK?

THINGS TO PRAY ABOUT (& NOT WORRY ABOUT)?

WHY DO I STILL NEED TO FINISH WHAT I STARTED?

NEW IDEAS, WISDOM, MINDSET SHIFTS:

THIS WEEK, I'M THANKFUL THAT I GET TO:

3 THINGS TO FINISH THIS WEEK:

MONDAY

PRIORITIES

TUESDAY

PRIORITIES

WEDNESDAY

PRIORITIES

FUEL TO FINISH: (PRAYERS, SCRIPTURE, MEMOS TO SELF...)

THURSDAY

PRIORITIES

_____
_____
_____
_____
_____

FRIDAY

PRIORITIES

_____
_____
_____
_____
_____

SATURDAY

SUNDAY

WEEKLY REFLECTION

HOW DID I FEEL ABOUT THIS WEEK?

ONE AMAZING THING THAT HAPPENED?

WHAT WILL I DO BETTER/DIFFERENTLY NEXT WEEK?

THINGS TO PRAY ABOUT (& NOT WORRY ABOUT)?

WHY DO I STILL NEED TO FINISH WHAT I STARTED?

NEW IDEAS, WISDOM, MINDSET SHIFTS:

THIS WEEK, I'M THANKFUL THAT I GET TO:

3 THINGS TO FINISH THIS WEEK:

MONDAY

PRIORITIES

TUESDAY

PRIORITIES

WEDNESDAY

PRIORITIES

FUEL TO FINISH: (PRAYERS, SCRIPTURE, MEMOS TO SELF...)

THURSDAY

PRIORITIES

FRIDAY

PRIORITIES

SATURDAY

SUNDAY

WEEKLY REFLECTION

HOW DID I FEEL ABOUT THIS WEEK?

ONE AMAZING THING THAT HAPPENED?

WHAT WILL I DO BETTER/DIFFERENTLY NEXT WEEK?

THINGS TO PRAY ABOUT (& NOT WORRY ABOUT)?

WHY DO I STILL NEED TO FINISH WHAT I STARTED?

NEW IDEAS, WISDOM, MINDSET SHIFTS:

THIS WEEK, I'M THANKFUL THAT I GET TO:

3 THINGS TO FINISH THIS WEEK:

MONDAY

PRIORITIES

TUESDAY

PRIORITIES

WEDNESDAY

PRIORITIES

FUEL TO FINISH: (PRAYERS, SCRIPTURE, MEMOS TO SELF...)

THURSDAY

PRIORITIES

FRIDAY

PRIORITIES

SATURDAY

SUNDAY

WEEKLY REFLECTION

HOW DID I FEEL ABOUT THIS WEEK?

ONE AMAZING THING THAT HAPPENED?

WHAT WILL I DO BETTER/DIFFERENTLY NEXT WEEK?

THINGS TO PRAY ABOUT (& NOT WORRY ABOUT)?

WHY DO I STILL NEED TO FINISH WHAT I STARTED?

NEW IDEAS, WISDOM, MINDSET SHIFTS:

"Finishing is better than starting."

– Ecclesiastes 7:8 (NLT)

WOMEN
WHO
FINISH

YOU WERE SAVED TO IMPACT YOUR CULTURE. LEAD. SERVE. WIN.
YOUR VOICE WILL SOUND DIFFERENT. DO NOT BLEND IN. STAND OUT.
FOCUS ON YOUR CALLING. IT'S THE ONLY ONE YOU'LL BE GOOD AT.
JUST START. USE YOUR TALENTS. DREAM. ASK. THEN BELIEVE.
YOU WERE GIVEN THE VISION. SO YOU PURSUE IT. DO IT AFRAID.
OBEY. MAKE DISCIPLES. EXPECT THE SUPERNATURAL. EXECUTE.
LAY ONE BRICK TODAY. EXALT CHRIST. THEN GET EXALTED BY GOD.
KNOW YOUR WHY. SOLVE A PROBLEM. MAKE $$. CREATE BEAUTY.
FAIL OFTEN. GRACE WORKS. CHOOSE PROGRESS OVER PERFECTION.

PRIORITIZE YOUR PURPOSE. CELEBRATE YOUR WINS.

BUT FIRST, FINISH.

Additional Notes

Additional Notes

Additional Notes

www.ingramcontent.com/pod-product-compliance
Lightning Source LLC
Chambersburg PA
CBHW060330100426
42812CB00003B/936